Manufacturing Management for Beginners

Basic tools for the first-time Manufacturing Supervisor

Written by
D.C. Rush

Manufacturing Management for Beginners

Table of Contents

Chapter One - Welcome to Management

Possibly, even a day earlier, you were a production worker, working alongside the employees you must now manage. You are probably friends with several of your coworkers and know them personally. You know their habits when it comes to being an employee such as which one misses time from work, who is habitually lazy or undriven. Who are the outstanding employees? You know them all.

After your company's vetting process, you were probably chosen from a small group of employees to manage or lead your department. You are qualified in your department and knowledgeable about the products you produce or the latest in manufacturing methods. What about management skills? Do you have experience or a degree in Management? Are you ready to accept this new responsibility, work long hours and dedicate yourself to the company you are working for? I can tell you firsthand that these are tough and real questions.

I was thrust into a management position. First, as a Production Supervisor and later as a Manufacturing Manager then a Plant Manager. I can tell you in the first days of being a Supervisor, I had the deer in the headlight expression most times. I was challenged, early and often.

Over my career, I was very pleased with my efforts to progress through the management ranks. I hope to give the reader a few skills that may help him or her through some real situations that might arise. You will be challenged but must remain in control if you plan to survive and ultimately succeed.

Chapter Two - Learning to Manage

I think it is very important to emulate a manager or supervisor you admire. I chose two General Supervisors I enjoyed working with. Any time either person asked me to take care of an issue, I always took care to get the job done and in a timely fashion. Both Supervisors were pleasant most times yet demanding where cost, quality, and delivery were concerned. I witnessed both Supervisors in action so to speak. When an employee crossed the line, they had a way to reprimand the employee yet not destroy their morale. That is a difficult thing to do. Even when terminating a person's employment, they were never mean-spirited, just direct, to the point and thorough. Most terminated employees knew well in advance they had crossed the line for one of several reasons, including absenteeism, quality, fraud, fighting, or just a lack of drive where their job was concerned.

I was challenged early. There was one friend who, before I became his supervisor, I would go out with after work to have a couple of drinks. I knew his family including his wife and children and vice versa, he knew mine. For some reason, this person felt he could coast once his friend, me, became the supervisor. He was dead wrong. My old friend began missing time from work and offered a halfhearted effort where his production quotas were concerned. I think it was a test. What should I do? I did not want to bother my manager with these concerns. After all, he might think I could not do my job. Nope, I had to go it alone.

I called my friend to the office for a chat. I did not document the conversation. This was probably a mistake. I would learn in future events to document the conversation with just a quick note and date, if nothing else, so I could prove I had a prior discussion with a particular employee.

I began talking with my friend, I'll call him Al.

I kept it light at first. Hi Al, how's the family doing? I wanted to show some empathy and keep things light. Al was a bit short with me. Al did not like being called upstairs to the office.

"What's going on," he said.

I began, "I first want to say I'm new to this job and I'll probably make mistakes. I hope you will support me in my job and understand I will have some difficult tasks to deal with, especially with people I know and admire." Sensing he was relaxing a little, I continued, "You are missing too much time from work. Other employees have brought this concern to my attention. Is something going on I can help you with?"

Al replied, "I am not doing anything I didn't do before you became the boss. What is your problem? I thought we were friends?"

I replied, "that is part of the problem. Outside of work, I may be your friend, but we are at work and we must follow company guidelines. That means both you and I must adhere to the attendance policy. Can you understand that?"

"Not really," Al replied. "It seems you are trying to use me to set an example."

"Look around," I said, "I am not documenting this conversation, although I probably should be doing so. It's because you are my friend outside of work. I don't want to cause you stress or embarrassment. I only need you to be the best employee in the department because other employees are watching us. Can you understand that"

"Yes, I think so," he replied. Al continued, "I'm not trying to take advantage of you because you and I occasionally do things outside of work. I will try harder to be here on time and give you my very best."

"Thanks very much," I responded. "One more thing, I will never tell anyone on the shop floor about this conversation. As far as I'm concerned, this is between you and me. If you want to tell someone, that is your business."

I discovered something very important that day. Whatever you do for one employee, you must do for everyone. For instance, when I brought an employee upstairs for an informal discussion, I would keep notes for myself but not formally document the conversation. If I took someone upstairs a second time, things were formally documented into a verbal warning and the employee signed showing they understood the context of the conversation along with anything they wanted to say on their behalf.

If an employee came to work feeling under the weather, I tried to put them on an easier job. I showed all the employees the same courtesy.

Chapter Three - Professional Courage

I was talking to one of my managers one day about an employee issue I was having. This employee liked wandering around and therefore his production was sub-par. He would leave his machine area often, talking to everybody. I made sure to walk past him on several occasions but that did not seem to deter him. My manager told me I needed to show some professional courage. That was a term I had never heard before but a lesson I would use many times in my career.

I wondered, what did he mean, professional courage? Was I afraid to do my job? No, I believed I could do my job but I didn't want to be mean-spirited. So, what to do?

I developed my management style. Whenever I saw this employee wandering away from his machine, I walked past him, making sure he noticed me. Then, a few minutes later, I would wander past him again. This time if the employee in question was still not at his machine, I would walk right up to him and tell him to get back to work. I thought to myself that he was forcing me to say something if he did not have the courtesy to return to his machine after the first time I walked past him. At that point, I felt it was appropriate to tell him to return to work and I was fine with that. That was my way of showing professional courage.

After a short time, when employees were not in their assigned work area, I would stroll around the area and take notes on who was absent from his or her assigned work area. Once they would see me, most time the employee automatically returned to work. Sometimes they did not. Here's an example of one of those times.

I'll call this operator James. I walked past James and he was off talking to a neighbor. When I returned for the second pass, he was still missing. I walked through the area and eventually found him, talking to a friend of his. In my mind, he was forcing me to do my job.

I began, "James, you need to get back to work."

James shot me a glance but continued talking to his friend.

"James, did you hear me? It's time to get back to work."

James responded, "I'm tired of you watching me all the time. Get off my back!"

I was not going to let James dictate the rules to me.

"James," I said, "I'm not picking on you or anyone else. Look around, everyone else is doing their job and it's time for you to go back to work."

James turned towards me and said, "I'll go back to work when you get back to your office!"

James was upset. What could I do? If I didn't do something, and fast, I could lose control of my entire department. I thought, OK this is a test and I do not plan to lose.

I said, "James, the machine you are scheduled to run is your current work assignment. If you refuse to go back to work, you will be considered insubordinate. If that happens, you can be immediately suspended and sent home pending a review by management and Human Relations where you could face further suspension or possibly termination."

James refused to return to work and told me he was not leaving work either.

James left me no choice. I called security and two guards escorted James out of the building, removing his badge pending an HR review. The following day James was terminated.

Now, that didn't make me happy. When James was on top of his game, he was a pretty good operator. Still, I couldn't allow James or any employee to challenge me, especially in front of others. Word got around pretty fast that James was terminated. Most of the employees understood since they knew the story. A few employees who were friends with James were a bit upset but deep down inside, even they understood James was wrong and that he brought this on himself. I found out that I did have professional courage and I could deal with any situation. Over the years I used my courage on occasion and I always remembered the first lesson I received from James.

Something to remember. If you have an insubordinate employee it is better if you have a witness. By witness, I mean another supervisor or manager. Have them come with you and be a witness when you give an employee an ultimatum. Afterward, make sure you and the witness document the

conversation as best you can, and sign and
date it.

Chapter Four - Performance Reviews

One of your most important jobs will be to write and deliver Performance Reviews. Reviews are typically given once a year. They usually are accompanied by a wage increase. Usually but not always. If the company is not performing well, there could be times when there is no money to hand out. Often, however, a small increase is given to keep up with inflation, say 3% to maybe 5%.

There was a time I managed nearly one hundred employees on the night shift. Talk about a lot of work writing and delivering that many reviews.

I can hear HR right now. Sometimes they demand you give everyone the same amount. Other times employees are rewarded based on performance. To me, performance-based increases are the best way to handle reviews. Occasionally HR will insist you do not give increases to those performing below standards. I don't like doing things this way. I prefer the company give me a pot of money to be used for Performance Review increases as I see fit. This way I can give those doing outstanding work a larger increase, something they can see on their paychecks. If I give someone a 6% increase, someone else may only get 2%. Before they leave the room, they will understand how they were reviewed and the reason for the small increase.

Writing reviews for outstanding employees are easy to write. Reviews for poor-performing employees can be challenging. Here is an example of an employee requiring improvement in several key areas.

Name: Bill

Attendance: Bill, you have missed eight days this past year. This is below the department average. An immediate and lasting improvement is required.

Quality: Bill, your quality has been very good. You take the time to check your parts often to make sure they fall within specifications. Keep up the good job!

Quantity: Bill, your quantity is far below department standards. You must stay in your assigned work area and avoid wandering to keep up your production output.

Overtime: Bill, you have accepted several overtime assignments this past year however you occasionally did not show up.

Area for Improvement: Bill, please remember once you accept overtime, missed assignments will count against your attendance.

Overall Performance: Bill, you are pleasant to work with. You are friendly and usually easy to talk with. Improvement in the areas noted is expected.

As you can see, Bill received decent marks for Quality however he needs improvement in other areas such as Attendance, Overtime, and Quantity of output of work. Once Bill leaves the room, he will understand how he is viewed and measured as an employee and what improvements are expected.

If in the coming month Bill has not shown any improvement, he will be formally documented with a verbal warning then possibly a written warning. These disciplinary actions could result in a suspension or even termination. Most time an employee will try to do better once they understand how the performance review can affect them and any potential wage increase.

Chapter Five - Management Styles

What kind of a supervisor would you like to be? To me, being known as a fair leader who is trusted by his employees and is known to go the extra mile for his subordinates is a great thing.

Here's how you begin the process. The easiest way is to manage by wandering around. Don't stay chained to your desk.

Make sure you walk through the department several times per shift. This serves a couple of things. First, the employees see you walking through the department. Knowing you may be walking around may help keep them at their machines or work areas. It also makes you available to your employees to answer any questions or concerns they might have. I learned right away to carry a small notebook with me so I could jot down questions from the employee. If you are sure to write down the question, you are less likely to forget. Employees appreciate it if you take the time to get back to them regarding a concern. Even if the answer is no, it's always better to let the employee know as soon as possible.

Let's say someone wants to take a day off, jot it down in your notebook. When you have a few minutes, check your employee calendar. If your calendar shows two employees already taking that day off, get back to the person who asked for the time off and explain to them why they cannot have the day off. They may not be happy but at least they have an answer. Maybe the employee can take an alternate day off or possibly one of the other two employees already scheduled to take that day off can change days.

One of the things I would try to keep track of are employee birthdays and other personal information such as the name of their spouse and children. When stopping by to chat with an employee I might ask how's Cathy doing instead of how his wife is doing. I always thought being personal with an employee worked better, at least for me.

Be pleasant! When you walk through the area keep an even temper. Even if you are stressed out there is no need to let the employees know about your troubles. It's probably no fault of theirs anyways.

Chapter Six - Department Improvements

Being a recognized leader in your company is very important. You should not feel the need to wait to make improvements in your work area. There are things you can do to make your department a showplace. You can do some of these improvements without going ballistic and upsetting your subordinates. One of these improvements is the implementation of 5-S.

You can begin implementation of the 5-S system in your department by taking small bites. When I taught 5-S we would completely shut down the entire area and go through the checklist, one by one. Shutting down production for a full shift did not please management. Keeping up with production is very important, therefore, I recommend going slow.

I'm also not an advocate of being rigid with the checklist. Once a machine or work area is clean, make sure it stays that way. An organized area will improve production and quality and especially with setup or changeover times.

Number 1 – SORT

Eliminate whatever is not needed by separating needed tools, parts, and instructions from unneeded materials.

Checklist

- Examples of items to remove from the work area
- Excessive amount of stock and supplies
- Tooling no longer needed
- Obsolete material
- Obsolete tooling
- Fixtures no longer needed

Be sure to check around the walls, corners, and on all surfaces including under benches, beneath desks, inside desk or bench drawers, inside cabinets, schedule boards, and tool boxes.

Number 2 – SET IN ORDER

Arrange items to assist efficient workflow and production.

Checklist

- Arrange the items you use most frequently close by
- Arrange tooling, fixtures, and other supplies in the order you will need them
- Keep only amounts of inventory necessary
- Specific items such as tooling and fixtures should be kept in designated areas
- Identify stored items with signs and labels

I'm a fan of using shadow boards. A shadow board typically has a place for most of the physical tools used at a machine or in a department. Every tool is easily identified. If everyone uses the board properly and returns the tools to the specified location, the shadow board looks nice and is very effective in removing clutter and organizing the tooling. Here's an example of a simple shadow board fabricated from a peg board.

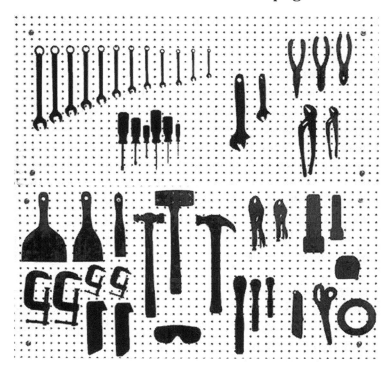

As you can see, building a shadow board is easy. Every tool has a place and they are easy to locate. Imagine people walking through your department and seeing all the tooling neatly displayed on a shadow board and not cluttering up the workbench.

Number 3 – Shine

Clean the machinery and work area so it is clean and tidy.

Checklist

- Clean the entire work area thoroughly
- Specify cleaning assignments
- Clean the work area as well as the walls, floors, and lighting fixtures
- Clean areas not normally seen such as under tables and on top of equipment and machinery

Keep a sufficient supply of cleaning supplies in designated areas including brooms, mops, cleaning solutions, and towels or rags.

Number 4 – Standardize

Document standards for a well-organized workplace.

Checklist

- Select team leader
- Determine rules and responsibility
- Management must provide ample time to properly incorporate 5S
- Management must provide guidance and support
- Workforce must embrace 5S principles and support the process in their work areas

Number 5 – Sustain

Maintain and review standards. This step is the most difficult process in the 5S system. After taking the time to sort, shine, set in order, and standardize, you would think sustaining would be easy however it is not. If not properly documented and maintained, the 5S system will most certainly fall apart.

Checklist

- Keep the entire team involved
- Reinforce the 5-S message as often as you can
- Provide leadership, resources, and time
- Be sure to recognize employee's efforts

Chapter Seven - Lean Tools

There are many tools you can use to improve quality, quantity, and thru-put in your manufacturing department. Most of these tools will take a great deal of time to input. You will probably need professional help depending on how far you plan to take these tools.

I would recommend implementing a couple of tools as you have time. Out of the twenty-five most common manufacturing tools, I have taken classes or live events with fourteen of these Lean Tools. You may or may not be familiar with some of the following tools. We have already discussed the 5-S System. In the end, I will give you an overview of additional tools you may be able to introduce into your manufacturing department with minimal disturbance.

- 5-S
- Bottleneck Analysis
- Continuous Flow
- Just-In-Time
- Kanban – Pull System
- Kaizen - Continuous Improvement
- Overall Equipment Effectiveness
- Poka-Yoke – Error Proofing
- Root Cause Analysis
- SMART Goals
- Standardized Work
- Takt Time
- Total Productive Maintenance
- Value Stream Mapping

Standardized Work

Standardized work is documented procedures for manufacturing that capture best practices, including the estimated time to complete each task. Following documented procedures helps eliminate waste by consistently applying best practices.

These instructions are designed to answer the following questions; How long should it take to change over a machine or process and how long to produce the first part while maintaining quality?

One example I like to use is the airplane checklist. Can you imagine the number of accidents there might be if pilots did whatever they wanted and in no specific order? The checklist is designed so any qualified pilot can follow procedures that enable them to safely take off or land their airplane. Each step is documented and in a specific order so that every pilot can get their passengers to their destination, on time and safely.

While your standardized work is not life-threatening it is still very important. We employed a lean coordinator. The coordinator would work alongside the employee to help document each step in making a changeover or setup. Once the employee and coordinator agreed on the work procedure, they signed off on the document and from then on, tried to follow it as closely as possible. It's amazing how much time you can save when people follow a standardized process every time.

Poka-Yokes

Poka-Yokes assist us with error-proofing the work area. Here are some examples where you already use error-proofing in everyday life.

- Car safety features
- Treadmills
- Microwaves, washing machines, dishwashers, and other household appliances
- Elevators & garage doors
- Leak-proof water bottles & travel mugs
- Power outlets and USB plugs
- Overflow outlets in sinks

Standardized work, 5-S, and Poka-Yokes are tools you can implement as you have time. It helps to have open-minded employees or associates, people who like to make an improvement that will ultimately make their jobs easier. Be sure to get input from your personnel. Make sure your employees embrace the change and are willing to help implement these tools.

This book and these suggestions are only a guideline. Please be sure to do the things you feel comfortable with. Develop your style. I wish you success and hope your journey is successful.

Chapter Eight - Quality

I've always found that improving quality is one of the most important things you can do. I went to work as a manufacturing manager for a company where it was acceptable to scrap the first couple of parts of each order. In the first year, the scrap rate was around 3.5%. So, for every one hundred parts produced, three or four parts could be scrapped out.

My immediate goal was to reduce the scrap rate by fifty percent each year. This goal was easily attained in the first year just by making sure the first part of each order was to specifications. By the end of the second year, we improved to just around one percent scrap.

Reducing scrap helped in several key areas. The cost of scrap was greatly reduced, saving the company money. Additionally, we reduced inventory. Bad things happen when you hold excessive inventory. Sometimes the parts in inventory or lost or damaged and they can also become obsolete.

About the Authors

To date, Donald and Cathy have written six children's books, illustrated in color and available in eBook, Paperback, and Audio. This novel, The Kirtland Killer, is their second full-length fiction crime suspense book.

Donald and Cathy live in Peoria, Arizona. Cathy is a homemaker and Donald is a retired Plant Manager and former Elementary Governing Board Member.

For additional information including ordering and social media links:

Website: www.dcrushbooks.com

Author Page: http://www.amazon.com/-/e/B00B0T04SI

Facebook: www.facebook.com/dcrushbooks

Pinterest: www.pinterest.com/dcrushbooks/

Twitter:

www.twitter.com/dcrushbooks

Linkedin:

www.linkedin.com/in/dcrushbooks

YouTube:

www.youtube.com/c/DCRush

Instagram:

www.instagram.com/dcrushbooks/